Even Crazier

HC
E. HORSLEY 3870

-3. FEB. 1989

-4 MAR 1989

22. MAR. 1989

25. APR. 1989

-6. MAY 1989

13 May 1989

23. MAY 1989

13 JUN 1989

18. JUL 1989

11. AUG. 1989

SURREY COUNTY LIBRARY
(Headquarters, West Street, Dorking.)
Charges will be payable at the Junior rate if this item
is not returned by the latest date stamped above.   L22A

Other Crazy joke books available in Beaver:

The Crazy Joke Book
More Crazy Jokes
The Craziest Joke Book Ever
Crazy Practical Jokes
Crazy Misstakes
Crazy Limericks
The Crazy Joke Book Strikes Back
The Crazy Crazy Joke Bag

EVEN CRAZIER JOKES

Compiled by Janet Rogers

Illustrated by Robert Nixon

Beaver Books

A Beaver Original
Published by Arrow Books Limited
62-65 Chandos Place, London WC2N 4NW
A division of Century Hutchinson Ltd
London Melbourne Sydney Auckland Johannesburg
and agencies throughout the world

First published in 1981
Sixth impression 1987
© Copyright text Victorama Limited 1981
© Copyright illustrations
Century Hutchinson Ltd 1981

This book is sold subject to the condition that it shall not, by way of trade or otherwise, be lent, resold, hired out, or otherwise circulated without the publisher's prior consent in any form of binding or cover other than that in which it is published and without a similar condition including this condition being imposed on the subsequent purchaser.

Set in Times

Printed and bound in Great Britain by
Anchor Brendon Limited, Tiptree, Essex

ISBN 0 09 952120 2

RODOLFO RUDOLPH, the red-nosed ringmaster, proudly presents his favourite jokes. . . .

RINGMASTER: *If this swelling on my legs gets any bigger, I won't be able to get my trousers on.*
DOCTOR: I'll give you something for it.
RINGMASTER: *What is it?*
DOCTOR: A prescription for a kilt.

An actor came into an agent's office and said: 'My act is really different. I can fly.'
　He then flew up to the ceiling, and after circling the room a few times he came down in a perfect landing.
　'Okay,' said the agent, 'so you do bird impressions. But what else can you do?'

Did you hear about the sword-swallower who swallowed an umbrella?
He wanted to put something away for a rainy day.

What do you get if you cross a cat with a ball of wool?
Mittens.

LITTLE BOY: *Do you know the difference between toffee and this old glove?*
RINGMASTER: No.
LITTLE BOY: *Good. Eat this old glove then!*

RINGMASTER: We regret to announce that the Invisible Man will not be seen tonight.

Knock, knock.
Who's there?
Ken.
Ken who?
Ken I come in?

RINGMASTER: *What was the name of that Man who had an act where he used to put his arm down a lion's throat?*
AGENT: I forget his name, but they call him 'Lefty' now.

Why does a monkey scratch himself?
Because he's the only one who knows where the itch is.

The most popular sideshow in the circus was a horse that played the bugle.
　A farmer who saw the show was amazed. He asked the horse's trainer how the horse had learned to play.
　'No mystery,' the trainer explained, 'he took lessons for years.'

Why does an ostrich have such a long neck?
Because its head is so far from its body.

Do you know the story about the empty glass? No?
There's absolutely nothing in it. . . .

DOCTOR: *And what's the matter with you, then?*
RINGMASTER: Water on the knee.
DOCTOR: *How do you know?*
RINGMASTER: I dropped a bucketful on it!

Why did the mother kangaroo scold her children?
Because they ate biscuits in bed.

My dog's got no nose.
How does he smell, then?
Pretty awful!

RINGMASTER: *Whatever happened to the lady you used to saw in half?*
MAGICIAN: Oh, she's fine. She's living in London and Birmingham.

Did you hear about the fat woman who went on a special diet.
All she ate for three months were coconuts and bananas.
After three months she hadn't lost any weight — but she couldn't half climb trees!

What did the dog say when it was scratched by the cat?
Nothing. Dogs can't talk.

Why did the bald man put a rabbit on his head?
Because he wanted a head of hare.

MAN: *My dog's alive with ticks.*
VET: Well, don't overwind him.

On which side does a chicken have most feathers?
On the outside.

SIMON (to his teacher): *I et seven eggs for breakfast this morning, Miss.*
TEACHER: You mean 'ate', Simon.
SIMON: *I only et seven.*
TEACHER: Ate.
SIMON: *Well, come to think of it, maybe it was eight eggs I et.*

What has a black cape, crawls through the night and bites people?
A tired mosquito with a black cape.

MAN: *I used to be in the circus.*
RINGMASTER: Oh, which cage were you in?

After a visit to the circus, George and Frank were discussing the thrills and marvels they had seen.

'I didn't think much of the knife-thrower, did you?' said George.

'I thought he was super!' enthused Frank.

'Well, I didn't,' said George. 'He kept chucking knives at that soppy girl and didn't hit her once!'

RINGMASTER: *I dreamed I had eaten a 20-pound marshmallow!*
DOCTOR: No need to worry, it was only a dream.
RINGMASTER: *Yes, but when I woke up my pillow was gone!*

BRUCE: *In Australia, I used to chase kangaroos on horseback.*
RINGMASTER: Well, I never, I didn't know kangaroos rode horses.

A Ringmaster looked out of his caravan one day on hearing the sound of music. On the street he saw an old man, a dog and a horse. The dog was playing an accordion, and the horse sang, while the old man collected money from the passers-by.

The Ringmaster was so impressed that he offered the trio a large sum of money to appear in his circus the following day. But when the day of the performance came they did not arrive, and were later discovered still playing on the street corner.

'What's the matter with you?' asked the Ringmaster. 'You could be earning a lot of money in the circus.'

'No. My conscience hurt me,' answered the old man.

'I didn't think it was fair to fool the public. The truth is, that horse can't sing. The dog's a ventriloquist.'

A man bought a ticket for the circus and went inside the tent. A moment later, he came out, bought another ticket and went in again.

This was repeated several times. Finally, when he bought his seventh ticket, the ticket-seller said: 'May I ask, sir, why you keep buying so many tickets?'

'There's a mad woman inside,' he answered. 'Every time I give her my ticket, she tears it up.'

Why do you want to leave the circus and work in a bank?
Well, I'm told there's money in it.

MIKE: *My brother's a puppeteer.*
PAUL: How did he get a job like that?
MIKE: *Oh, he pulled a few strings.*

I just sat down on a pin.
Did it hurt?
No, it was a safety pin.

IAN: *My Mum took me to the circus last night.*
BRIAN: Did you like it?
IAN: *No, I cried.*
BRIAN: Why, was it sad?
IAN: *No, we couldn't get in.*

On their way to the seaside to perform in the circus, a trainer and his talking dog were speeding along in a brand new sports car. Suddenly a police car started closing in on them.

'You'd better pull up on the side of the road,' the dog told the trainer. 'And remember — when he gets here, let me do the talking!'

Where does a 500-pound elephant sleep?
Where it wants to!

If a man was born in Italy, raised in Australia, came to England, and died in America, what is he?
Dead.

Two singers were about to enter the circus ring when one of them burst into a mad fit of coughing.
 'Anything wrong?' asked the other.
 'I think I've got a frog in my throat,' gasped the first.
 'Then if I were you I should let the frog sing – it's got a much better voice than you.'

What do you get if you cross a hedgehog with a giraffe?
A ten-foot toothbrush.

DOCTOR: *And what is your problem?*
RINGMASTER: I prefer brown socks to green socks.
DOCTOR: *What's the problem? Lots of people do, even me.*
RINGMASTER: Phew! What a relief! How do you like yours — fried or boiled?

A magician used to perform his magic act on board a luxury cruise ship each evening. Also on board the ship was a parrot which belonged to one of the sailors. Every time the magician started his act the parrot would scream:

'Phoney! Phoney!'

One day, however, the ship sank and all that remained was the parrot sitting on one end of a plank and the magician on the other. The parrot turned to the magician and said:

'Okay, clever, what did you do with the ship?'

What would you get if you crossed a cocker, a poodle and a rooster?
A cockerpoodledo.

CLOWN: *What is the equator?*
RINGMASTER: I don't know.
CLOWN: *An imaginary lion running round the earth.*

What do you get if you cross a squirrel with a kangaroo?
An animal that carries nuts in its pocket.

LION-TAMER: *One of my lions swallowed a flash-light last night.*
RINGMASTER: Is he all right?
LION-TAMER: *Yes, he's fine. He spat it out this morning, and now he's delighted.*

What kind of animals in a circus can jump higher than a house?
All of them. Houses can't jump.

Why are four-legged animals such poor dancers?
Because they have two left feet.

What did the beaver say to the tree?
Its been nice gnawing you.

What reptile is very good at mathematics?
An adder.

What is the biggest ant in the world?
A Gi-ant.

Did you hear about the little boy called Dad?
They named him after his father.

What breakfast cereals do witches like best?
The ones that go snap, *cackle*, pop!

What is always dressing?
Salad cream.

RINGMASTER: *You have got your boots on the wrong feet!*
CLOWN: No I haven't, these are the only feet I've got.

What is black and white and noisy?
A zebra with a set of drums.

Why do little witches always get A's at school?
Because they're so good at spelling.

BABY CHICK: *What did I say when I found an orange in my nest?*
RINGMASTER: I don't know, what did you say?
BABY CHICK: *Look what marmalade!*

A goat was in a rubbish dump looking for food. He discovered a can of film and very quickly ate it. Another goat came along and asked if the film was any good.

'It was all right,' replied the goat, 'but I preferred the book.'

What has no legs but always walks?
A pair of shoes.

Which is the left side of a pie?
The piece that is left over.

Knock, knock.
Who's there?
Alison.
Alison who?
Alison to my radio.

FIRST BOY: *My new digital watch is broken.*
SECOND BOY: How do you know?
FIRST BOY: *It's stopped ticking.*

GIRL (watching a film): *Oh, wasn't that thriller exciting. It sent a cold slithery lump down my spine.*
BOY: Oh gosh! So that's where my ice-cream went.

What has three feet but cannot walk?
A yard.

PASSENGER: *Does this bus stop at the river?*
CONDUCTOR: If it doesn't there'll be a very big splash.

There was once a little boy who had a turned-up nose.
Every time he sneezed he blew his school cap off.

A mother heard her daughter giggling and whispering with her friends in the bedroom. So she called:
    'What are you doing, children?'
    'We're playing at churches,' came the reply.
    'Well, you shouldn't giggle and whisper in church, should you?'
    'Oh, we're the choirboys.'

What happened to the little boy who ran away with the circus?
The police made him bring it back.

Why is the man who worked as a human cannon-ball not at the circus any more?
Because he was discharged.

What did the polar bear have for lunch?
Iceburgers.

How do you keep a skunk from smelling?
Hold his nose.

Do you know the story of the three holes in the ground?
Well, well, well. . . .

GIRL: *What does your dad do for a living?*
BOY: He works in a flea circus.
GIRL: *What does your mum do?*
BOY: Scratch.

If you fed a cow money would you get rich milk?

MAN TO FRIEND: *My dog doesn't eat meat.*
FRIEND: Why not?
MAN: *I never give him any.*

What is a barbecue?
A row of men waiting to have their hair cut.

What did one arithmetic book say to the other?
I've got a big problem.

VICAR: *You must not fight, little boy. You should love your enemy.*
BOY: But he's not my enemy. He's my brother.

Does a cow give milk?
No, you take it from her.

WOMAN TO GIRL: *And where is your little brother?*
GIRL: He's in the house playing a piano duet. I finished first.

BOY: *What's cold, white and very high, with a summit and ears?*
GIRL: I don't know.
BOY: *A mountain.*
GIRL: Where's its ears?
BOY: *Haven't you heard of mountain-ears?*

How do you keep an idiot in suspense?
I'll tell you next week.

'*Mummy, all the kids say I look like a werewolf.*'
'Shut up and comb your face!'

When a man put his head into the lion's mouth to see how many teeth it had, what did the lion do.
The lion closed its mouth to see how many heads the man had.

Why did Simple Simon put corn in his shoes?
Because he had pigeon toes.

GAMEKEEPER: *Oi! There's no fishing allowed here.*
JOHNNY: I'm not fishing, I'm just washing my pet maggot.

Did you hear about the boy who does bird impressions?
He eats worms.

PASSENGER: *Is this bus going to Clapham?*
CONDUCTOR: Only if they're good enough, sir.

What is worse than being with a fool?
Fooling with a bee.

Why do dragons sleep during the day?
So that they can fight knights.

Extract from a letter written by a fond mother to her son:
　Your Auntie Betty's just had her teeth out and a new fireplace put in. Well, I must write quickly now because my pen's running out. . . .

PEPE and PEPITA, Europe's nimblest acrobats, present their favourite jokes. . . .

What did the bean plant say to the farmer?
Stop picking on me.

PEPE: *Who was Captain Kidd?*
PEPITA: He was an acrobat.
PEPE: *What do you mean he was an acrobat?*
PEPITA: It says in this book that he often sat on his chest.

Why does Lucy like the letter K?
Because it makes Lucy Lucky.

What is the best year for a kangaroo?
A leap year.

PEPE: *Why do skunks argue?*
PEPITA: I give up. Why?
PEPE: *Because they like to raise a stink.*

What's the difference between a mad king and a street?
One tosses crowns, the other crosses towns.

PEPE: Pepita uses lemon juice for her complexion. No wonder she always looks so sour!

Why are cemeteries so very popular?
Because people are dying to get in!

Who has feathers, fangs and goes quack?
Count Duckula.

How does a monster count to 19?
On its fingers.

PEPE: *So what, he spreads happiness wherever he goes.*
PEPITA: I said *wh*enever he goes.

A man went into a butcher's shop and was horrified to see human arms and legs of all sizes hanging on hooks.
　'Why, that's horrible!' he cried.
The butcher scowled at him:
　'Well, what did you expect to see in a family butcher's shop?'

Where do snowflakes dance?
At the snowball.

PEPE: *I know a restaurant where we can eat dirt cheap.*
PEPITA: Who wants to eat dirt?

What did the tree say to the axe?
I'm stumped.

PEPITA: *Have you had your dinner yet?*
PEPE: Yes, I was so hungry at seven fifty-nine that I eight o'clock.

What did one invisible man say to the other invisible man?
It's nice not to see you again.

Did you hear about the cannibal who went for a cruise on a luxury liner?
At dinner he refused the menu and asked for the passenger list.

NAVAL OFFICER: *Can you swim?*
RECRUIT: Why, have you run out of ships?

What's black when clean and white when dirty?
A blackboard.

PEPITA: *People keep telling me I'm beautiful.*
PEPE: They must have vivid imaginations!

LADY CRABTREE: *I suppose this old picture is meant to be a work of art?*
ANTIQUE DEALER: Actually, modom, that is a mirror.

PEPE: *My hair is getting thinner.*
PEPITA: Who wants fat hair anyway?

What did the pencil say to the rubber?
Take me to your ruler.

What time of day was Adam created?
Just before EVE.

MRS JONES: *I finally got my son to stop biting his nails.*
MRS SMITH: How did you manage that?
MRS JONES: *I made him wear shoes.*

What do you do with a green monster?
Wait until he's ripe.

What's worse than raining cats and dogs?
Hailing taxis.

PEPE: *Why is a cat longer at night than in the morning?*
PEPITA: Because he's let out every night and taken in again every morning.

STRANGER: *Catch any fish?*
FISHERMAN: Did I? I took thirty out of this stream this morning.
STRANGER: *Do you know who I am? I'm the gamekeeper.*
FISHERMAN: Do you know who I am? The biggest liar in the country!

Adam and his son Cain were walking in the fields when the boy asked:
'Who was that lady I saw you with last night?'
'That wasn't night, that was Eve,' answered Adam.

Did you hear about the French horn player whose wig fell into his instrument? He spent the rest of the concert blowing his top.

Where do frogs sit?
On toadstools.

What is a prickly pear?
Two porcupines.

Why is it difficult to keep a secret in the North Pole?
Because your teeth tend to chatter.

SCIENCE TEACHER: *Can anyone tell me — what is bacteria?*
DOPEY DIANA: It's the rear entrance to a cafeteria.

Why does a Hallowe'en witch ride on a broom?
So that she can sweep the sky.

PEPE: *Where do you take your baths?*
PEPITA: In the spring.
PEPE: *I said 'where', not 'when'.*

Why do witches fly on broomsticks?
It's better than walking.

What is the difference between an acrobat and a duck?
One goes quick on her legs, the other goes quack on her legs.

Who does a fiend see every Saturday night?
His girl fiend.

Did you hear the story about Algy and the bear? It's very short. Algy met a bear. The bear was bulgy. The bulge was Algy.

PEPE: *Why did the rat gnaw a hole in the carpet?*
PEPITA: Tell me. Why?
PEPE: *He wanted to see the floor show.*

'Can I have a chemistry set?' asked baby skunk.
'No,' said his mother, 'it'll make the house smell.'

PEPE: *I've just discovered the tightrope-walker's secret.*
PEPITA: How did you find out?
PEPE: *By tapping his wire.*

An acrobat is a very useful person to know – he's always capable of doing a good turn and will bend over backwards to help you.

What starts with E, ends with E, and has one letter in it?
An envelope.

Why did the chicken cross the road?
For fowl reasons.

What did the invisible girl want to be when she grew up?
A gone-gone dancer.

What does Santa Claus do when it's not Christmas?
He is probably a farmer because he always says: 'Hoe, hoe, hoe!'

Why don't bananas snore?
They don't want to wake up the rest of the bunch.

PEPE: *Did you ever hear the memory joke?*
PEPITA: No.
PEPE: *Sorry, I've forgotten it.*

Why are tightrope-walkers like book-keepers?
Because they know how to balance.

POLICEMAN: *I see that one of the tyres on your caravan is bald.*
PEPE: O.K. I'll see it gets some 'air.

Why is the Lone Ranger rich?
Because he always rides on Silver.

If a quadruped has four legs and a biped has two legs, what is a zebra?
A stri-ped.

MUM: *Who is that at the door?*
CHARLIE: A man with a wooden leg.
MUM: *Well, tell him to hop it.*

What animals are mathematical?
Rabbits, because they multiply so well.

PEPE: *Where are English Kings and Queens usually crowned?*
PEPITA: On their heads, silly.

Do you sell dog's bones?
Only if they are with an adult.

Why do Eskimos weep so much?
Each Eskimo must have his daily blubber.

PEPITA: *I haven't slept for days.*
PEPE: *Why not?*
PEPITA: *Because I sleep at night!*

What did the man say when he tried to rob a glue factory?
This is a stick-up!

What's the difference between a lame bull and a lumberjack?
One hops and chews, the other chops and hews.

PEPE: *I'm going to Bury St Edmunds today.*
PEPITA: Why? Is he dead?

A man entered a crowded doctor's waiting-room, fell to the ground, rolled himself into a ball and started tumbling around the room. Soon patients, furniture and magazines were flying everywhere. The noise brought the doctor running from his surgery.
   'What on earth's the matter with you?'
   'I'm a billiard ball,' said the man.
   'Well,' said the doctor, 'you'd better come to the head of the queue.'

How does a ghoul begin a letter?
Tomb it may concern.

Why are false teeth like stars?
Because they come out at night.

PEPE: *Do you know why the football stadium is so cool?*
PEPITA: No, why?
PEPE: *Because it is full of fans.*

DOCTOR: *You have a very bad cold. I advise you to avoid draughts for a few days.*
PATIENT: Can I play snakes and ladders instead?

Where do motorists usually get punctures in their tyres?
At forks in the road.

What is a contented cannibal?
Someone who is fed up with people.

PEPE: *Did you hear about the man who fell out of a ten-storey block of flats?*
PEPITA: Did he hurt himself?
PEPE: *No, he only fell from the ground-floor window.*

What is the difference between a cat and a flea?
A cat can have fleas, but a flea can't have cats.

Why are stamps such weaklings?
Because they are always taking a licking.

PASSENGER: *Does this bus go to Crewe?*
CONDUCTOR: No.
PASSENGER: *It says so on the front.*
CONDUCTOR: There's an advert for baked beans on the side, but we don't sell them.

What do geese eat?
Gooseberries.

What do ghosts have for tea?
Spookhetti on toast.

DOCTOR: *You must take things quietly.*
PATIENT: I do — I'm a burglar!

MAN TO FRIEND: *My dog has no tail.*
FRIEND: How do you know when he's happy?
MAN: *When he stops biting me.*

Why does a cowboy take a hammer to bed?
So that he can hit the hay.

BOY: *How far is your home from the school?*
GIRL: Only ten minutes walk if you run.

What do you get when you cross a cow with a camel?
Lumpy milkshakes.

What is it that you and every person in the world has experienced but will never see again?
Yesterday.

CUSTOMER: *I want a dress to match my eyes.*
SALESGIRL: Sorry, madam, we don't sell bloodshot dresses.

Why do men stay away from the letter A?
Because it makes men mean.

PEPE: *I hear that egg shampoo is good for your hair.*
PEPITA: But how do you get a hen to lay an egg on your head?

MRS BLOGGS: *Is your mother at home, Willy?*
WILLY: You don't think I'm cutting the grass because it's long, do you?

GUEST: *It's nice, but I would prefer a room with a bath.*
HOTEL MANAGER: This is not your room, sir, this is the lift.

PEPE: *I stayed in a hotel that advertised 'Bed and Board'.*
PEPITA: Was it all right?
PEPE: *Yes, except I never knew which was the bed and which was the board.*

DOCTOR: *There's nothing wrong with you, you're just lazy.*

PATIENT: Can you give me the medical term for it so that I can tell my friends what I'm suffering from?

TONI, TRIXI and TOSCA, those daredevil trick cyclists from Italy, come wheeling in with their favourite selection. . . .

TOSCA: *Have you heard the story of the dirty shirt?*
TONI: No.
TOSCA: *That's one on you.*

TRIXI: *How can you tell twin witches apart?*
TONI: It's not easy to tell witch is witch.

What animal talks a lot?
A yak.

31

Which animal talks the most?
A yakety-yak.

Why do squirrels spend so much time in trees?
To get away from all the nuts on the ground.

TONI: *I bet I can make you say 'black'.*
TOSCA: Okay, try it.
TONI: *What are the colours of the Union Jack?*
TOSCA: Red, white and blue.
TONI: *I told you I'd make you say 'black'.*
TOSCA: I didn't say 'black'.

Knock, knock!
Who's there?
A little kid who can't reach the bell.

Where does satisfaction come from?
A satisfactory.

TRIXI: *I lose something every time I stand up.*
TOSCA: What?
TRIXI: *My lap!*

Why is a book like a king?
They both have pages.

What is the difference between a counterfeit pound note and a crazy rabbit?
One is bad money, the other is a mad bunny.

What season is it when you are on a trampoline?
Spring time.

TONI: *What is a fast tricycle?*
TOSCA: I don't know. What?
TONI: *A tot rod.*

One day while riding through a thunderstorm, the cyclist got a puncture outside a monastery. A monk came out and invited him inside to have dinner and spend the night. The cyclist accepted because it was very wet outside and he had a long way to go before reaching the next town. That night he was given a wonderful meal of fish and chips. He decided to compliment the chef, so he went into the kitchen and asked the cook:

'Are you the fish friar?'

'No,' the man replied, 'I'm the chip monk.'

What happened when the American stoats got married?
They became the United Stoats (States) of America.

What is the difference between someone who's just been bitten by a mosquito and a trick cyclist about to enter the circus ring?
One is going to itch, the other is itching to go.

Why are pianos so noble?
Many are upright, the rest are grand.

What did the little light bulb say to its mother?
I wuv you watts and watts.

What goes up and down but never moves?
A flight of stairs.

What did the plank of wood say to the electric drill?
You bore me.

CUSTOMER: *Waiter, there's soap in this food!*
WAITER: That's to wash it down with, sir.

Why is it easy to break into an old man's house?
Because his gait is broken, and his locks are few.

When travellers climb to the top of the Great Pyramid, what kind of joke do they find there?
A cone-under-'em.

Why is the letter T like an island?
Because it is in the middle of water.

What is the difference between a greatcoat and a baby?
One I wear, the other I was.

What is the difference between a blind man and a sailor in prison?
One can't see to go, the other can't go to sea.

What did the boy centipede say to the girl centipede?
'You sure have a nice pair of legs, pair of legs, pair of legs. . . .'

What animal has death no effect on?
A pig, because as soon as you have killed him you can cure him and save his bacon.

How many skunks do you need to make a big stink?
A phew.

When is a woman not a woman?
When she is a little chilli (chilly).

When is a girl not a girl?
When she is a bell (belle).

When is a man not a man?
When he is a bed (abed).

Why did the invisible man look in the mirror?
To see if he still wasn't there.

TRIXI: *Isn't it wonderful how little chicks get out of their shells?*
TONI: It's more wonderful how they get in.

'There's a man outside with a wooden leg called Smith.'
'Oh, and what's his other leg called?'

What is the difference between a market-gardener and a billiard maker?
One minds his peas, and the other minds his cues.

TOSCA: *A snake just snapped at me.*
TONI: *Don't be silly, snakes don't snap.*
TOSCA: *This one did, it was a garter snake.*

What is the difference between influenza and photography?
One makes facsimiles, the other makes sick families.

An elephant always remembers, but what kind of an animal always forgets?
An owl, because it keeps saying 'Who? Who?'

TRIXI: *Did you hear the story about the peacock?*
TONI: Yes, it's a beautiful tail (tale).

Why is a sow a sow?
Because 'at's how she is (a sow she is).

TONI: *Have you ever caught German measles?*
TOSCA: No, I've never been to Germany.

What is the easiest way to make a banana split?
Cut it in half.

TOSCA: *Where was Solomon's temple?*
TONI: On the side of his head!

Why is a tight shoe like a fine summer?
Because it makes corn grow.

An Eskimo mother was sitting in her igloo reading nursery rhymes to her young son:
'Little Jack Horner sat in a corner. . . .'
'Mum,' interrupted the boy, 'what's a corner?'

What is the poorest plant?
A vine, because it can't support itself.

TONI: *We just flew in from Italy.*
RINGMASTER: I bet your arms are tired.

TRIXI: *Why do you always carry a compass around with you?*
TOSCA: So I know whether I'm coming or going.

Why is hot bread like a caterpillar?
Because it is the grub that makes the butter fly.

Where is it that everyone is beautiful?
In the dark.

When is a black dog not a black dog?
When he is a greyhound.

TONI: I heard a good joke and was going to take it home, but I decided that that was carrying a joke too far.

What is the difference between an accepted lover and a rejected lover?
One kisses his missis, the other misses his kisses.

TONI: *Why did the Secret Agent talk into the hairdryer?*
TOSCA: *I don't know, why?*
TONI: *Because it was a short wave radio.*

What fish sings songs?
A tuna fish.

When is a blow from someone perfectly acceptable?
When they strike you agreeably.

What is the loudest sport?
Tennis, because everyone raises a racket (racquet).

What is the difference between a soldier and a bombshell?
One goes to war, the other goes to peaces (pieces).

TRIXI: *Have you heard what the sea said to the shore?*
TONI: No, what?
TRIXI: *Nothing. It just waved.*

What is purple and 5000 miles long?
The Grape Wall of China.

TOSCA: *Do moths cry?*
TRIXI: Certainly, haven't you ever seen a mothball (bawl)?

Why is 'yes' the most ignorant word in the English language?
Because it doesn't 'no' anything.

EXAMINER: *It seems to me that you know very little, if anything, about the Bible. Is there any passage you can repeat?*
STUDENT: Judas departed and went and hanged himself.
EXAMINER: *Very good, perhaps you will repeat another.*
STUDENT: Go thou and do likewise.

What is a panther?
Someone who makes panths.

What is a tongue twister?
When your tang gets all tongueled up.

What is the difference between an attempted murder and the butchering of swine?
One is assault with intent to kill, and the other to kill with intent to salt.

What is the best day for making pancakes?
Fry-day.

When is a man not a man?
When he turns into a street.

TRIXI: *What has nothing left but a nose when it loses an eye?*
TONI: I haven't a clue. What's the answer?
TRIXI: *No-i-se.*

Why did the biscuit cry?
Because its mother had been a wafer so long.

There was once an Indian Chief whose name was Shortcake. He lived with his wife Squaw high up in the mountains. Sadly, one day Shortcake died and a very sympathetic Indian asked Squaw what she was going to do with him. She answered mournfully: 'Squaw bury Shortcake.'

TONI: *I dreamt that I danced with the world's most beautiful girl.*
TRIXI: What was I wearing?

Why is a freshly picked carnation like a children's illness?
Because it is a new pink off (an whooping cough).

What is the teapot's favourite song?
'Home on the Range.'

What runs across the floor with no legs?
Water.

When is a clock on the stairs dangerous?
When it runs down.

If you cross a bee and chopped meat, what do you get?
A humburger.

What smells most in a chemist's shop?
Your nose.

'Doctor, Doctor, I've got carrots growing out of my ears!'
'How on earth did that happen?'
'I don't know – I planted cucumbers.'

TONI: *What is the difference between an Irishman frozen to death and a Scotsman at the North Pole?*
TOSCA: I've no idea, what?
TONI: *One is killed with the cold, the other is cold with the kilt.*

What are arithmetic bugs?
Mosquitoes, because they *add* to misery, *subtract* from pleasure, *divide* your attention, and *multiply* quickly.

LEO, LOLA, LANA and LULU, the fearsome, ferocious, but fun-loving lions from the wilds of Africa, hope to make you roar at their favourite jokes. . . .

What do you get if you cross a canary with a lion?
I don't know, but when it sings you'd better listen!

What are the best steps to take when you meet a lion?
Very big ones.

Did you hear about the scientist who crossed a parrot with a lion?
It bit off his arm and said 'Who's a pretty boy!'

August was the name of a puppy who was always picking on larger animals. One day he got into an argument with a lion. The next day was the first of September. Why?
Because that was the last of August.

FIRST HUNTER: *It's getting very late. We haven't hit a single lion all day.*
SECOND HUNTER: Let's just miss a couple more and go home.

What's a skeleton?
Bones with people scraped off.

A nasty big lion was walking around the circus ring. The first animal he met was a monkey. The lion pounced on the poor monkey and roared: 'Who's the greatest animal in this circus?' The frightened monkey replied: 'You are, O mighty lion!' So the lion let him go.

The next animal he met was a performing seal. He pounced on the seal and roared: 'Who is the greatest animal in this circus?' The frightened seal replied: 'You are, O mighty lion!' So the lion let him go too.

The lion then met an elephant and asked the same question. The elephant grabbed the lion, twirled him around, and then threw him fifty feet into the air.

Picking himself up off the ground the lion dusted himself down and said:

'There's no need to get rough just because you don't know the answer.'

What's the difference between a thunderstorm and a lion with a sore paw?
One pours with rain, and one's paw makes him roar with pain.

What do you get if you cross a lion and a monkey?
A swinging lion.

LION-TAMER: *Don't worry, this lion will eat off your hand.*
LITTLE BOY: That's what I'm worried about.

FUNNY MAN: *I was surrounded by lions in the park this morning.*
BOY: By lions!
FUNNY MAN: *Yes, dandelions.*

TIM: *I don't like having my face washed.*
MUM: Well, you'll have to do it when you grow up.
TIM: *No, I won't, I'll grow a beard.*

What is a ghost's favourite rock?
Tomb stone.

Why was the girl dancer in the circus called Sugar?
Because she was so refined.

Why does the lion kneel before it springs?
Because it is preying.

If you were surrounded by ten lions, four tigers, three bears and four leopards, how would you escape?
Wait until the merry-go-round stopped and get off.

What do you get if you cross a lion with a kangaroo?
A fur coat with pockets.

Why shouldn't you grab a lion's tail?
It may only be his tail, but it could be your end!

What do hippopotamuses have that no other animals have?
Baby hippopotamuses.

What did the lion say when it saw two hunters in a jeep?
'Meals on wheels. . . .'

'*Would you rather a lion ate you or a gorilla?*'
'I would rather the lion ate the gorilla.'

What lion never moves?
A dandelion.

HE: *Would you like me to put my head into the lion's mouth.*
SHE: Yes.
HE: *And I thought we were friends.*

HORACE: *This is a beautiful stuffed lion.*
MAURICE: Yes, I shot it in Africa while on a hunting expedition with my uncle.
HORACE: *What is it stuffed with?*
MAURICE: My uncle.

What puzzle makes you very angry?
A crossword puzzle.

What do you get if you cross a lion with a mouse?
MIGHTY MOUSE!

What animal breaks the law?
A cheetah.

'*Mum, what is a vampire?*'
'Shut up, and drink your soup before it clots.'

EX-CIRCUS LION FOR SALE, FULLY-TRAINED, FAITHFUL, WILL EAT ANYTHING, ESPECIALLY FOND OF CHILDREN.

Why is the letter A like a flower?
Because a B comes after it.

Who is bigger, Mrs Bigger or her baby?
Her baby is a little bigger.

Why did the owl in the circus make everyone laugh?
Because he was a howl.

What would you do if a friend told you he had killed a thirteen-foot lion in Africa?
Tell him that is some lyin'.

What is higher than a circus tent and seems smaller than a mouse?
A star.

HE: *I think the laundry must have sent me the wrong shirt. The collar is so tight I can hardly breathe.*
SHE: Don't be silly, you've got your head through a button-hole.

Did you hear about the lion with pedestrian eyes?
They look both ways before they cross.

LEO LION: *I'm going to sneeze.*
LANA LION: Who to?
LEO LION: *At-choo.* . . . (At you).

FATHER TO SON: *If you fall out of that tree and break both your legs don't you come running to me.*

What is the main ingredient in dog biscuits?
Collie flour.

'I wish lions were born without teeth!'
'They usually are!'

What is the difference between a sick horse and a dead bee?
One is a seedy beast, the other a bee deceased.

POSH LADY: *Little boy, will you help me look for my dog with one eye?*
TOMMY: I'd rather use both my eyes, lady.

BARBER: *Was your tie red before you came in, sir?*
CUSTOMER: No.
BARBER: *Oh dear!!*

BOY: *Mum says I should have been born in Hungary.*
GIRL: Why?
BOY: *Because I'm always hungry.*

What fur did Adam and Eve wear?
Bearskins.

DOCTOR: *What is the trouble?*
PATIENT: I think I'm a lion.
DOCTOR: *How long has this been going on?*
PATIENT: Ever since I was a cub.

What grows bigger the more you take from it?
A hole.

What did the coke say to the coal?
'What kind of fuel am I?'

How many lions would fit into an empty circus ring?
One, after that it isn't empty any more.

How do you find a lost rabbit?
Make a noise like a big carrot.

What is worse than toad-in-the-hole?
A frog in the throat.

What English king had a heart transplant?
Richard the first, because when he became a crusader he was said to have the heart of a lion.

What is a cheerful flea?
A hoptimist.

LOLA LION: *Where do fleas go in winter?*
LULU LION: Search me.

A lion-tamer went to hospital after being bitten on the leg by a lion.

'Did you put anything on it?' asked the nurse.

'No,' replied the lion-tamer, 'he liked it just the way it was.'

What happened to the cannibals when they ate a comedian?
They had a feast of fun.

What happens when you eat yeast and polish?
You rise and shine!

What do you say when you meet a two-headed monster?
Hello – hello.

Why are dogs like trees?
They both have barks.

How can you tell if a bucket is not well?
If it looks a little pale (pail).

What belongs to you but is used more by other people?
Your name.

What do you get if you cross a zebra with an ape man?
Tarzan stripes forever.

The lady named her cat 'Trouble'. One night it sneaked out of the house, the lady was so worried that she went out searching for it in her nightgown.

She ran into her local police-station, and when asked what she was doing out at that hour dressed only in her nightgown she said:

'I'm looking for Trouble.'

BOY: *I'm so glad you named me Joe.*
MOTHER: Why do you say that?
BOY: *Because that's what all the kids at school call me.*

TEACHER: *Can you tell me what happened in 1896.*
BOY: I can't even remember what happened last night.

MAN: *What do you do when you see a big lion?*
LION-TAMER: Hope he doesn't see me.

What sort of animals use nut-crackers?
Toothless squirrels.

What animal do you look like when you take a bath?
A little bear.

I know a hairdresser who breeds dogs. I don't know what sort they are, but he says they're shampoodles.

What has six legs, four ears and a tail?
A man on a horse.

'*I say, waiter, this soup tastes funny!*'
'So why don't you laugh?'

JIMMY: *My dad came across a snarling lion in the jungle and didn't turn a hair.*
TIMMY: I'm not surprised – your dad's bald!

As one ghost said to another ghost: 'I'm sorry, but I simply don't believe in people.'

LEN: *They arrested the sword-swallower and now he's in jail.*
KEN: What did he do?
LEN: *He hiccoughed and stabbed two people.*

PROUD MOTHER: *Ever since Sammy was a little boy he has always wanted to work in a circus and saw people in half.*
FRIEND: Is he your only child?
PROUD MOTHER: *No, he has several half brothers and sisters.*

LONG DISTANCE RUNNER: *There's something wrong with my feet.*
DOCTOR: Oh, yes, it looks like athlete's foot.

TEACHER: *If I had thirty apples in one hand and forty in the other, what would I have?*
TONY: Big hands.

What is the longest night of the year?
A fortnight.

What words can be pronounced quicker and shorter by adding another syllable to them?
'Quick' and 'Short'.

'Doctor, Doctor, everyone thinks I'm a liar!'
'I don't believe you.'

What is pink, lives at the bottom of the ocean and sings 'Give me the moonlight'?
Frankie Prawn.

'Have you ever seen a man-eating lion?'
'No, but I've seen a man eating fish and chips.'

Where were potatoes first found?
In the ground.

DOCTOR: *How did you get that splinter in your finger?*
PATIENT: All I did was scratch my head.

What is oil before it is pumped out of the ground?
A well-kept secret.

WIFE: *We're having mother for dinner, dear.*
HUSBAND: Oh, I'd rather have sausages.

JUDGE: *Order, order in court!*
PRISONER: I'll have a ham sandwich.

Why is the letter G like the sun?
Because it is the centre of light.

FIVE STAR JOKES

JACKY, JIMBO, JOLLITO, JAN AND JAVEY, five jovial jugglers, toss in their own favourite jokes. See if you can catch them. . . .

JAVEY: *What lives in winter, dies in summer, and grows with its roots upwards?*
JAN: What?
JAVEY: *An icicle.*

JOLLITO: *I woke up this morning feeling awful. My head was spinning, and everything was going round and round.*
JIMBO: You must have slept like a top.

What kind of umbrella does the Queen carry on a rainy day?
A wet one.

What has two eyes like a juggler, arms like a juggler, hands like a juggler, but isn't a juggler?
A photograph of a juggler.

What examination do farmers take?
Hay levels.

JAVEY: *I'd like to tell you a joke about the measles.*
JIMBO: I don't think you should.
JAVEY: *Why not?*
JIMBO: Well, you know how these things spread.

Why is a boy scout like a tin of fruit?
They are both prepared.

What gallops down the road on its head?
A horseshoe nail.

JAN: *Did anyone laugh when you slipped on the ice?*
JACKY: No, but the ice made some awful cracks.

Why do girls look at the moon?
Because there's a man in it.

Which is the fastest animal, the otter or the beaver?
The 'otter of the two.

JACKY: *What did the baby porcupine say when he backed into a cactus?*
JAN: Is that you, Ma?

What goes through a door, but never goes in or out?
A keyhole.

'Waiter! This plate is wet.'
'Sir, that is your soup.'

MOTHER LION: *What are you doing, son?*
LION CUB: *I'm chasing a hunter round a tree.*
MOTHER LION: *How many times must I tell you not to play with your food?*

Where do cows go on holiday?
Moo York.

What famous dance music did Charles Dickens write?
'Oliver Twist'.

JACKY: *Did you hear about the rabbit with a lisp who went to the dentist to get a tooth extracted?*
JOLLITO: No.
JACKY: *The dentist asked him if he wanted gas, and the rabbit answered, 'No, I'm an ether bunny.'*

What kind of coat can you only put on when it's wet?
A coat of paint.

What fish is famous?
A star-fish.

The mother turkey was scolding her children for being naughty.
'You bad children,' she said, 'if your father could hear you he'd turn over in his gravy.'

What's the longest piece of furniture in the world?
A multiplication table.

GHOUL FRIEND: *My goodness, hasn't your little ghoul grown!*
GHOUL MOTHER: Yes, she's certainly gruesome.

What is the distance between a stupid person's ears?
Next to nothing.

WAITER: *How did you find your steak, sir?*
CUSTOMER: I just moved a potato and there it was.

JACKY: *I call my girlfriend Peach.*
JAVEY: Why? Because she's so sweet?
JACKY: *No, because she has a heart of stone.*

Did you hear about the karate champion who joined the army?
The first time he saluted he nearly killed himself.

Where do butchers dance?
At the meatball.

Jock came back home to Edinburgh after a visit to London.
 'It's a lovely place,' he told his friend, 'but they've got some very strange customs. Every night they knocked on my bedroom wall, then on the ceiling, then on the floor. Sometimes I could hardly hear my bagpipes!'

Did you hear the story about a piece of butter?
Well, I don't want to spread it around.

What did one angel say to the other angel?
'Halo.'

Two ants were exploring a supermarket. They climbed up on a shelf and on to a box of cornflakes. Suddenly the first ant began running.
 'Wait for me!' cried the other ant. 'What's the hurry?'
 'Can't you read?' said the first. 'It says here: TEAR ALONG THE DOTTED LINE.'

What did the mother bee say to the naughty baby bee?
'Just behive yourself.'

JACKY: *I say, Jollito, why has that cycle got flat tyres?*
JOLLITO: So that I can reach the pedals.

Why did the rooster refuse to fight?
Because he was a chicken.

What man is strong enough to hold up a car with one hand?
A policeman.

JIMBO: *I've got a wonder watch. It only cost me £1.*
JACKY: What's a wonder watch?
JIMBO: *Every time I look at it I wonder if it's still going.*

Our kitchen is so small that we only use condensed milk.

Why are ghosts simple things?
Because they can easily be seen through.

What is the astronaut's favourite meal?
Launch.

'*Your Dad's shaved his beard off again, that's the third time this year!*'
'Yes, it's because of Mum. She's stuffing a cushion.'

TEACHER: *Hold your hand out, Brown, I'm going to give you the cane.*
BROWN: Thank you, sir, what shall I do with it?

Why shouldn't you cry when a cow falls on the ice?
Because it's no good crying over spilt milk.

What do you call a cat who sucks lemons?
A sourpuss.

How do you get the police in Australia?
Dial 666.

Where does Superman get the food he needs to make him so big and strong?
At the supermarket.

JOLLITO: *Do you think I'm vain?*
JACKY: Of course not. Why do you ask?
JOLLITO: *Well, other girls as beautiful as me usually are.*

Which will burn longer: the candles on the birthday cake of a boy or the candles on the birthday cake of a girl?
Neither, candles burn shorter, not longer.

Why did the glow-worm at the circus get so upset?
She didn't know whether she was coming or glowing.

What is the difference between a person who gossips and a dog?
One has a wagging tail, the other a wagging tongue.

Knock, knock.
Who's there?'
Godfrey.
Godfrey who?
Godfrey tickets for the circus tonight.

JACKY: *Did you hear about the two blood cells?*
JAVEY: No, what happened?
JACKY: *They loved in vein.*

Who invented the first aeroplane that wouldn't fly?
The Wrong Brothers.

What sort of song would a ghost sing?
A haunting melody.

What is the difference between an umbrella and someone who never stops talking?
The umbrella can be shut up.

What is double-glazing?
A man with glasses who's had too much to drink.

What is the biggest moth in the world?
A mam-moth.

What did the necklace say to the hat?
You go on ahead, I'll just hang around.

What's yellow and writes?
A ball-point banana.

What kind of book does Frankenstein like to read?
One with a cemetery plot.

What is always coming, but never arrives?
Tomorrow.

Where would you find a prehistoric cow?
In a Moo-seum.

JACKEY: *Why are you standing on your head?*
JAVEY: Just turning things over in my mind.

What did the laundry-man say to the impatient customer?
'Keep your shirt on.'

What did one escalator say to the other?
I think I'm coming down with something.

TEACHER: *Spell the word 'needle', Kenneth.*
KENNETH: 'N-e-i—'
TEACHER: *No, Kenneth, there's no 'i' in needle.*
KENNETH: Then it's a rotten needle, Miss!

What kind of doctor treats a duck?
A quack doctor.

JOLLITO: *Why is your arm in a sling?*
JIMBO: I get all the breaks.

JAVEY: *Why did you bury your old car?*
JAN: Well, the battery was dead, the pistons were shot, and then the engine died.

Why are there no psychiatrists for dogs?
Because they aren't allowed on couches.

Why was the musician arrested?
He got into treble.

TEACHER: *Kenneth, you're late for school.*
KENNETH: I sprained my ankle, Miss.
TEACHER: *That's a lame excuse.*

How do you write 'fifty miles under the sea' in four words?
$$\frac{\text{the sea}}{\text{fifty miles}}$$

What is the difference between a coyote and a flea?
One prowls on the prairie, the other prowls on the hairy.

What is green and noisy and very dangerous?
A herd of pickles.

Why do so few people play the harp?
It takes a lot of pluck.

CANNIBAL MOTHER (*to son*): Just because your father was tough when he was alive, there's no need to leave him on the side of your plate.

JAVEY: *What did one balloon say to the other balloon?*
JIMBO: What?
JAVEY: *Nothing. Balloons can't talk.*

Have you heard the story about the church bell?
It hasn't been tolled (told).

JACKY: *Excuse me, officer, I've lost my dog.*
POLICEMAN: Come back tomorrow, we might have a lead on him.

When things go wrong what can you always count on?
Your fingers.

MEL: *I can lie in bed and watch the sun rise.*
BEL: So what, I can sit in the kitchen and watch the kitchen sink.

Why is the ocean angry?
Because it's been crossed so many times.

What holds the moon up?
Moon beams.

HUSBAND: *Anything good on telly, dear?*
WIFE: Only your tea, I put it on top to keep warm.

Why are seeds like gateposts?
Because they propagate.

Why does Father Christmas always come down the chimney?
Because it soots him.

Why is it rude to whisper?
Because it is not aloud (allowed).

JAN: *How does a coffee-pot feel when it's full?*
JACKY: Perky.

'It looks like rain.'
'I know it does, but it said Chicken Soup on the packet.'

TEACHER: *Did you make someone happy today?*
NAUGHTY NIGEL: Yes, I went to see my aunt and when I left she was happy.

AUNT LUCY: *And what are you going to give your brother for his birthday?*
IRIS: Don't know. Last year I gave him the measles.

SIX STAR JOKES

Now those world-famous performing HORSES gallop into the ring to trot out their favourite jokes....

Why doesn't it cost very much to feed a circus horse?
Because a horse eats best when it doesn't have a bit in its mouth.

LITTLE BOY: *Dad, there's a man at the circus who jumps on a horse's back, slips underneath, catches hold of its tail and finishes on the horse's neck!*
FATHER: That's nothing. I did all that the first time I rode a horse.

What colour was Napoleon's white horse?
White.

Who always goes to bed with shoes on?
A horse.

Where do you take a sick horse?
Horsepital.

Why did the bareback performer in the circus ride his horse?
Because it got too heavy to carry.

Why is a good-tempered horse not likely to be a very good jumper?
Because it won't easily take offence (a fence).

What cat lives in the ocean?
An octopuss.

What game do horses like playing best?
Stable-tennis.

Why was the horse all charged up?
Because it ate haywire.

How do you spell 'hungry horse' in just four letters?
M.T.G.G.

If a horse loses its tail where does it get another?
At a re-tail shop.

What horse can you put your shirt on and make sure you get it back?
A clothes horse.

A city dweller came to a farm and saw a very beautiful horse. He decided that he must have the animal, so he bargained with the farmer, and finally got it for a very high price.

The city man jumped on the horse and shouted:
'Giddyup!' but the horse didn't move a muscle.
The farmer explained:
'This is a very special horse, he used to work in a circus and he'll only move if you say "Praise the Lord" to him. To stop him, you have to say "Amen".'

Keeping this in mind the city man yelled: 'Praise the Lord!' at the top of his voice, at that the horse took off with very great speed and headed off towards a cliff.

The rider panicked, and only just in time remembered to shout 'Amen!' at which the horse came screeching to a halt right at the edge of the cliff.

Feeing very relieved, the rider raised his eyes to heaven and exclaimed:
'Praise the Lord!'

Why do bees hum?
Because they don't know the words.

'My pet kangaroo can't wait until 1984.'
'Why not?'
'It's leap year!'

CUSTOMER: *Have you any wild duck?*
WAITER: No, sir, but we can take a tame one and irritate him for you.

'Show me a polka-dot pony, and I'll show you a horse of a different colour.'

KENN: *What is the best way to mount a horse?*
BENN: How should I know? I'm not a taxidermist.

A man walked up to the delivery window of a Post Office where a new clerk was sorting out the mail.

'Anything for Mike Howe?' asked the man.

The clerk ignored him so he repeated the question in a very loud voice. Without looking up the clerk replied:

'No, none for your cow, and none for your horse either!'

FIRST TRAINER: *That last race was a very close finish. Did you think your horse had won?*
SECOND TRAINER: Yes, but when I saw the photo finish the answer was in the negative.

'Did you hear that big noise this morning?'
'Yes, was it the crack of dawn?'
'No, it was the break of day.'

The thunder god went for a ride on his favourite horse.
'I'm Thor!' he cried.
The horse replied:
'You forgot the thaddle, thilly.'

What is a nightmare?
A horse who stays up very late.

Why was the little pony unhappy?
Because every time it wanted something, its mother would say 'Neigh'.

What is horse sense?
Just stable thinking.

What is a big game hunter?
A football fan who's lost his way to the match.

Why is a carpenter like a pilot?
Because they both know all about planes.

Where did Columbus stand when he discovered America?
On his feet.

Why did the farmer take the cow to the vet?
Because she was moody.

What do you call a pony with a sore throat?
A hoarse horse.

A circus trainer was riding his horse around the circus ring when a little dog jumped into the ring and shouted:
 'Hello, there!'
 'Hello,' replied the surprised trainer, 'I didn't know that dogs could talk.'
 His horse turned his head and said:
 'You learn something new every day, don't you?'

What is the difference between a sleeping horse and one that is awake?
With some horses it is difficult to tell!

Two Irishmen bought a horse each at a sale in Dublin. Both horses were similar so Sean said to Patrick:
 'How shall we tell the horses apart?'
 'Oi tell you what,' said Patrick. 'We'll bob the tail of one of them.'
 But by mistake both the tails got bobbed so that they were still in the same predicament.
 'Oi know what we'll do,' said Sean. 'You take the black one and Oi'll have the whoite one!'

What goes further the slower it goes?
Money.

What goes through water, but doesn't get wet?
A ray of light.

What is a horse's favourite song?
'Big Horse (because) I love you.'

A man's car suddenly stopped dead when he was driving down the middle of a country lane. He stepped out of the car and looked inside the bonnet to see if he could fix it.
　After a while a horse ambled up beside him, had a look at the car and said:
　'Your trouble is probably in the carburettor.'
　The man was so amazed that he ran down the road until he met the farmer walking towards him. He stopped the farmer and told him exactly what had happened.
　'Did the horse have a white patch in the middle of his forehead?' asked the farmer.
　'Yes, yes!' cried the motorist.
　'Don't pay any attention, then,' said the farmer, 'that was only old Dobbin and he doesn't know a thing about cars.'

What is avoidance?
A dance for people who hate each other.

SQUIRE: *Is there anything I can do for you, sire?*
KING ARTHUR: Yes, make haste and fetch a can opener. I have a flea in my knight clothes.

Why was the cowboy a lot of fun?
Because he was always horsing around.

TED: *I just had ten rides on a Merry-Go-Round.*
NED: You really get around, don't you!

FARMER: *That's a very small egg.*
POULTRYMAN: It was only laid yesterday, give it a chance.

What happens to old horses?
They become nags.

Do mountains have ears?
Yes, they are mountaineers.

Why did the horse chase its tail?
To make both ends meet.

Why aren't horses well dressed?
Because they wear shoes, but no socks.

PATIENT: *Doctor, I'm not feeling well.*
DOCTOR: What seems to be the trouble?
PATIENT: *I work like a horse, eat like a bird, and I'm as tired as a dog.*
DOCTOR: Sounds as if you need a vet more than a doctor.

CUSTOMER: *Waiter, there's no turtle in this turtle soup!*
WAITER: Of course not, and there's no horse in the horseradish either.

RIDER: *I wanted to go one way and the horse wanted to go the other.*
FRIEND: What happened?
RIDER: *We tossed for it.*

FRED: *I can lift a horse with one hand.*
TED: I bet you can't.
FRED: *Show me a horse with one hand and I'll lift it.*

What are assets?
Little donkeys.

What did one horse say to the other horse?
'I forget your name, but your pace is familiar.'

Why couldn't the astronauts stay on the moon?
There wasn't any room. It was a full moon.

What is the difference between a biscuit and a horse?
You can dip a biscuit in your tea, but you can't fit a horse into the cup.

EILEEN: *Mum, do you water a horse when it's thirsty?*
MUM: Yes, dear.
EILEEN: *Then I'm going to milk the cat.*

'Our cat is very smart. It eats a piece of cheese and then breathes down a mousehole.'

'If a horse's head is pointing north, where would its tail be pointing?'
'To the south?'
'No, to the ground.'

BENN: *Why do you call your horse Sonny?*
KENN: Because he is so bright.

Why are lollipops like racehorses?
Because the more you lick them the faster they go.

A very mean man went into a saddler's shop and asked for one spur.
　'Why only one?' asked the saddler.
　'Because if I can get one side of the horse to go, the other side is sure to come with it.'

Three men were in a boat. It capsized. Only two got their hair wet. Why?
The third one was bald.

Why is it hard to talk with a goat around?
Because it always butts in.

'Why did you throw away your alarm clock?'
'It always went off while I was asleep.'

Why did the man hit the dentist?
Because he got on his nerves.

What is empty during the day and full at night?
Your bed.

'Stop acting like a fool.'
'I'm not acting.'

What is dark but made by light?
A shadow.

How can you tell when a train has gone?
It leaves tracks behind.

Why was the horse so polite?
Every time he approached a fence he let the rider go first.

Why is one day never complete?
Because it always begins by breaking.

'Please call me a taxi.'
'OK, you're a taxi, but you look more like a bus to me.'

Why are vampires crazy?
Because they are often bats.

Why are clouds like people riding horses?
Because they hold the reins (rains).

What did Baby Corn say to Mother Corn?
Where is Pop Corn?

What part of a fish weighs the most?
The scales.

What two things should you never eat before breakfast?
Lunch and supper.

'Doctor, what's good for biting finger-nails?'
'Sharp teeth.'

If Fortune had a daughter, what would she be called?
Mis-fortune.

A little boy was taken to the circus for the first time. When he saw the horses he asked:
   'Dad, where are their rockers?'

'How have you been getting on with horse riding?'
'I've been taking a running-jump.'

What has four legs and can't walk?
Two pairs of trousers.

What's brown and can see just as well from either end?
A horse with its eyes shut.

SEVEN STAR JOKES

Seven slinky SEALS slip into the circus and proudly present their favourite jokes. . . .

What was Noah's profession?
He was an ark-itect.

A man took a seal into a very large department store in London and started to get into the lift. The lift operator said to the man:
　'Sorry, sir, but you can't bring that seal in here.'
　'But I have to,' said the man, 'he gets dizzy on the escalator.'

'Dad, I don't want to go to Australia. . . .'
'Shut up, and keep digging.'

When was it always wet in France?
When the monarchs were reigning (raining).

What question can you never answer 'Yes' to?
'Are you asleep?'

Why did the baker stop baking bread?
Because he wasn't making enough dough.

Why is money sometimes called dough?
Because we all knead it.

What is the difference between a railway engine in its shed and a tree?
One leaves its shed, the other sheds its leaves.

What is the dirtiest word in the world?
Pollution.

WIFE: *Have you put the cat out?*
HUSBAND: Yes – I've just trodden on his tail.

What did Benjamin Franklin say when he discovered electricity in lightning?
Nothing – he was too shocked.

Did you hear about the optician who fell into the lens-grinding machine and made a spectacle of himself.

MUM: *Carol, why are you crying?*
CAROL: Judith just broke my doll!
MUM: *How did she break it?*
CAROL: I hit her on the head with it.

GIRL SEAL: *I'm burning with love for you.*
BOY SEAL: Come now, don't make a fuel of yourself.

Why is a daily paper like an army?
Because it has leaders, columns and reviews.

What did the log say?
'I slept like a human last night.'

Can you telephone from an aeroplane?
Yes, the plane is the one without a dial.

What kind of bath can you take without water?
A sunbath.

What is bigger when it is upside down?
The number 6.

SAMMY SEAL: *My brother reminds me of a space-rocket.*
SIDNEY SEAL: Why do you say that?
SAMMY SEAL: *He's off his rocker.*

What did the first tonsil say to the second tonsil?
The doctor's taking me out tonight.

SIDNEY SEAL: *My sister has a photographic memory.*
SAMMY SEAL: That must be very useful.
SIDNEY SEAL: *Not really, nothing ever seems to develop.*

Why can't you tell a story about a bed?
It hasn't been made yet.

SAMMY SEAL: *Do you like seed cake?*
SIDNEY SEAL: Don't know, I never seed any.

What does a seal become after it is six months old?
Seven months old.

What did the bee say to the flower?
'Hello, honey.'

KENN: *Have you ever studied blotting paper?*
BENN: No.
KENN: *It's very absorbing.*

Should you eat chicken with your fingers?
No, fingers should be eaten separately.

Why is an old car like a classroom?
Because it contains a lot of nuts, with a crank up front.

What puts the white lines on the ocean?
An ocean liner.

What can travel at the speed of sound, but has neither wheels, wings, nor an engine?
Your voice.

Little Averil's mother thought she was beginning to show off too much, so one night when guests came for dinner, Mother said:

'If Averil comes in and tries to attract your attention just don't take any notice of her. She's supposed to be in bed.'

It was not long before Averil appeared in her nightgown and walked around the room. The guests did as they were told and pretended not to see her. After a while Averil returned to her bedroom, looking very pleased with herself.

Next morning her Mother overheard Avril saying:

'It worked. Last night I rubbed on Mum's vanishing cream and nobody saw me.'

When do broken bones make themselves useful?
When they begin to knit.

What did the pen say to the paper?
'I dot an "i" on you.'

What can you serve, but never eat?
A tennis ball.

Did you hear about the Secret Agent who made explosives?
He made a bomb.

VEGETARIAN: *I've lived on vegetables for years.*
BORED FRIEND: So what? I've lived on earth all my life.

Why is a drama teacher like the Pony Express?
Because he is a stage coach.

What is the most shocking city in the world?
Electri-city.

Why does lightning shock people?
It doesn't know how to conduct itself.

KENN: *Isn't Mother Nature wonderful?*
BENN: Why?
KENN: *Well, millions of years ago she didn't know man was going to invent glasses, but look where she put our ears.*

How do you make a sausage roll?
Push it.

Who was the world's first underwater spy?
James Pond.

How do you make a Maltese Cross?
Set fire to the tails of his shirt.

What did the woman say to the adding machine?
I'm counting on you.

What do Eskimos call their money?
Iced lolly.

How can you tell an undertaker?
By his grave manner.

What could you do if you were on a desert island with no food or water?
   Open up your watch and drink from the spring and eat the sandwich is there (sand which is there).

Why should a sailor know where the biggest seals live?
Because he's been to sea (see).

What word allows you take away two letters and get one?
Stone.

Why is breakfast in bed so easy?
It's just a few rolls and a turnover.

Why is rugby football like bread?
Because of its scrums (its crumbs).

What is black and white and red all over?
A sunburnt zebra.

How do we know Rome was built at night?
Because Rome wasn't built in a day.

What is a parrot stuffed with?
Pollyfilla.

How should you treat a baby goat?
Like a kid.

Why is the letter D like a bad boy?
Because it makes Ma mad.

What is an autobiography?
The life story of an automobile.

What has a hundred limbs but can't walk?
A tree.

What is a fund for poor musicians?
A band aid.

Why is a sinking ship like a person in gaol?
They both need bailing out.

What would the time be if a lion ate a postman?
8 p.m. (ate p.m.).

FIRST ESKIMO: *How odd! I put radiators in my kayak and it went up in flames. Why?*
SECOND ESKIMO: Simple, you can't have your kayak and 'eat it.

When is spanking like a hat?
When it is felt.

MUMMY SEAL: *Why are you making faces at that bulldog?*
LITTLE SEAL: He started it.

If five seals catch five fish in five minutes, how long would it take one seal to catch one fish?
Five minutes.

What happened when Abel died?
He became unable.

What is hypnotism?
Rheumatism in the hip.

What did one mountain say to another mountain after an earthquake?
That wasn't my fault.

'*Dad bought Mum a mink outfit for her birthday.*'
'*Cor! Did he?*'
'*Yes, two steel traps and a shotgun.*'

TEACHER: *If a straight line is the shortest distance between two points, what is a bee line, Carol?*
CAROL: The shortest distance between two buzz stops.

When is a farmer cruel?
When he pulls the ears off corn.

MAN: *Why do you call your umbrella Adam?*
WOMAN: Because one of its ribs is missing.

When does it rain money?
Whenever there's a change in the weather.

What is the Spook's navy called?
The Ghost Guard.

MINNIE: *Why are your hands shaking?*
WINNIE: I suppose they must be glad to see each other.

SHOPKEEPER: *Do you wish to buy a Japanese radio, Sir?*
CUSTOMER: No thank you, I don't understand the language.

What kind of robbery is not dangerous?
A safe robbery.

What do you get when you feed lemons to a cat?
A sour puss.

POLICEMAN: *Didn't you see the 30 mph sign?*
DRIVER: No, I was going too fast to see it.

Why do footballers wear shorts?
Because they would be arrested if they didn't.

MAN: *I didn't know your wife could dance so well.*
HUSBAND: She can't. The waiter spilled soup in her lap.

What animal goes skin-diving?
A mosquito.

TRAMP: *Will you give me some money for a cup of coffee?*
MAN: No thanks, I don't like coffee.

VICTIM: *They stole everything from my house except the soap and towels.*
FRIEND: Why, the dirty crooks.

What do you call a bee born in May?
A maybe.

When was the clock at its most dangerous?
When it struck twelve.

What did the buffalo say to his son when he went away on a long trip?
'Bison!'

Where do hogs keep their money?
In piggy banks.

If cheese comes on top of a hamburger, what comes after cheese?
A mouse.

KENN: *I fell and hit my head against a piano.*
BENN: Did you hurt yourself?
KENN: *No, I hit the soft pedal.*

Why do large cars go quickly?
Because they've got a big boot behind.

ANGEL: *How did you get to heaven?*
NEW ARRIVAL: 'Flu.

What kind of tables do people eat?
Vege-tables.

EIGHT STAR JOKES

Eight enormous ELEPHANTS enter the ring to present their favourite jokes and give you a gigantic laugh....

How can you tell if there's an elephant sleeping in your bed?
Look for peanut shells.

ANIMAL TRAINER: *I went riding this morning.*
RINGMASTER: Elephant back?
ANIMAL TRAINER: *Oh yes, he got back just before me.*

Why are Egyptian children good children?
Because they repect their mummies.

LITTLE GIRL: *Mummy, why are your hands so soft?*
MOTHER: Because I always use wonderful new Cleanshine Liquid for washing my dishes.
LITTLE GIRL: *But why does it get your hands so soft?*
MOTHER: Because the money Cleanshine Liquid pay me for this commercial enables me to buy an automatic dishwasher.

KENN: *Why did you become a printer?*
BENN: I was the right type.

What is big and grey and mutters?
A Mumbo-Jumbo.

Why is the letter E lazy?
Because it is always in bed.

MRS OWL: *I'm worried about baby owl.*
MR OWL: *Why?*
MRS OWL: *He doesn't give a hoot about anything.*

What did one tooth say to the other tooth?
'There's gold in them there fills.'

A woman sat on a bus eating peanuts. Trying to be friendly she offered some to the woman who was sitting beside her.
   'Goodness, no!' said the second woman, 'peanuts are fattening.'
   'What makes you think that?' asked the first.
   'My dear! Have you ever seen a slim elephant?'

What do you call Eskimo cows?
Eskimoos.

Why did the elephant paint himself all different colours?
So he could hide in a crayon box.

How do you tell an elephant from a monster?
A monster never remembers.

What's grey, has four legs, and a trunk?
A mouse going on holiday.

What is worse than a giraffe with a stiff neck?
An elephant with a blocked nose.

What did the big toe say to the little toe?
There's a big heel following us.

What has four legs and flies?
A dead elephant.

Why does a mother carry her baby?
Because the baby can't carry its mummy.

INQUIRER: *I want to put an advertisement in your newspaper.*
TELEPHONIST: Is it to go in the Small Ads, sir?
INQUIRER: *Heavens, no. I want to sell an elephant.*

What did the protoplasm say to the amoeba?
'Don't bacilli.'

TEACHER: *Ivan, where is Felixstowe?*
IVAN: On the end of Felix's foot.

Where can you find cards on a ship?
On the deck.

Did you hear about the elephant who went to the seaside to see something new in trunks?

What do you call an elephant that flies?
A Jumbo Jet.

Why did the orange stop?
Because it ran out of juice.

Why did the jelly roll?
It saw the apple turnover.

What did the elephant rock star say into the microphone?
'Tusking, tusking – one, two, three, tusking.'

What goes when the wagon goes, stops when it stops, is of no use, but a wagon cannot get along without it?
A squeak.

Did you hear about the sword-swallower who went on a diet?
He had pins and needles for months.

'More than six thousand elephants go each year to make piano keys.'
'It's amazing what animals can be trained to do.'

PATIENT: *Can a person be in love with an elephant?*
DOCTOR: No.
PATIENT: *Do you know anyone who wants to buy a very large engagement ring?*

What did Tarzan say when he saw the elephants coming?
Here come the elephants.

What did Tarzan say when he saw the elephants coming with sunglasses on?
Nothing. He didn't recognise them.

BIG ELEPHANT: *What are you doing with a pencil and paper?*
LITTLE ELEPHANT: I'm writing to my brother.
BIG ELEPHANT: *But you don't know how to write.*
LITTLE ELEPHANT: That's O.K., he can't read.

What did the elephant think of the grape's home?
De-vine.

How does an elephant get out of a tree?
He climbs on a leaf and waits for Autumn.

ALF: *I'm worried about my brother, he thinks he's a lift.*
DOCTOR: Send him up.
ALF: *I can't, he doesn't stop at your floor.*

Where was the Magna Carta signed?
At the bottom.

STRONGMAN: *I am so strong I can tear up a telephone directory.*
LITTLE BOY: That's nothing, yesterday my brother ran out of the house and tore up the street.

What did the river say when the elephant sat on it?
Well, I'm dammed.

What did the dirt say to the rain?
If this keeps up my name will be mud.

When do ghosts haunt skyscrapers?
When they are in high spirits.

What do monsters sing at Christmas?
'Deck the halls with poison ivy. . . .'

Where do you learn how to work in an ice-cream parlour?
At sundae school.

What's the difference between an elephant and a banana?
You can peel a banana, but have you ever tried peeling an elephant?

VISITOR: *What's the name of your new baby elephant?*
KEEPER: I don't know. He won't tell me.

What is white on the outside and grey on the inside?
An elephant sandwich.

JOHN: *Why do elephants paint their toe-nails red?*
MARK: I don't know, why?
JOHN: *So that they can hide in the strawberry field.*
MARK: I don't believe that.
JOHN: *Have you ever seen an elephant in a strawberry field.*
MARK: No!
JOHN: *See? It works!*

HE: *What is the difference between an elephant and a mattababy?*
SHE: What's a 'mattababy'?
HE: *Nothing, dear, what's the matter with you?*

What do you have to know to teach an elephant tricks?
More than the elephant.

ELEPHANT TRAINER: *Doctor, my elephant has swallowed a bullet, what shall I do?*
DOCTOR: Just don't point him at anybody.

DOCTOR: *What is the problem?*
TRAINER: My elephant has swallowed a roll of film.
DOCTOR: *Don't worry, nothing serious will develop.*

MIKE: *You play draughts with an elephant? He must be very clever.*
STEVE: Not really. I beat him most of the time.

What time is it when an elephant sits on your fence?
Time to get a new fence.

When things go wrong, what can you always count on?
Your fingers.

What do you get if you cross an elephant with a mouse?
Great big holes in your skirting board.

A small girl was telling her friend about a visit to the circus.

'And I saw the elephants,' she said. 'Guess what they were doing?'

'I don't know,' replied her friend.

'Picking up peanuts with their vacuum cleaners.'

In the final seconds of a circus football match it looked as if Freddy the Flea was going to score a goal and win the game when suddenly Enid the Elephant, on the defending side, trod on Freddy and squashed him as flat as a pancake.

The referee blew his whistle.

'You've killed him!' he shouted. 'I'll have to send you off!'

'But I didn't mean to kill him, I only meant to trip him up!'

Can a match box?
No, but a tin can.

What's the difference between an Indian elephant and an African elephant?
About 3000 miles.

MUM: *Who was that at the door?*
SAMMY: A woman with a pram.
MUM: *Tell her to push off.*

What did one pencil say to the other?
I've got a leadache.

WIFE: *I want that dress in the window.*
HUSBAND: It is in the window already.

What makes the hearse hoarse?
The coffin (coughin').

What do you get if you cross a bug with the Union Jack?
A patrio-tick.

WAITER: *How would you like your steak, sir?*
CUSTOMER: Big, please.

What speaks all the languages of the world?
An echo.

Where in France do all the houses have two bathrooms?
Toulouse.

Why is an elephant grey, large and wrinkled?
Because if it were small, white and round it would be an aspirin.

Why couldn't the elephants go swimming together?
Because they only had one pair of trunks between them.

How can you tell if there's an elephant in your oven?
You can't shut the door.

'Doctor, Doctor, I keep seeing elephants with yellow spots.'
'Have you ever seen a psychiatrist?'
'No, only elephants with yellow spots.'

What would you do with a blue elephant?
Take him to the circus and cheer him up.

What is big, grey and too dangerous even to appear in a circus?
An elephant with a machine gun.

Who is Tarzan's favourite singer?
Harry Elephante.

What is worse than a turtle with claustrophobia?
An elephant with hay fever.

When the biggest elephant in the world fell down a well, how did it get out?
Wet.

Why did the elephants leave the circus?
They were tired of working for peanuts.

What do you do with old bowling balls?
Give them to elephants to play marbles.

What did the digital watch say to the clock?
Look, no hands!

'Waiter, there's a button in my salad.'
'I expect it fell off, sir, whilst the salad was dressing.'

What is the shortest bridge in the world?
The bridge of your nose.

BOY: *Why do you call your boyfriend 'Laryngitis'?*
GIRL: Because he's a pain in the neck.

Why is the letter 'F' like a cow's tail?
Because it's at the end of beef.

MAN: *Is this letter yours? The name is smudged.*
NEIGHBOUR: It can't be mine, my name is Smith.

HUSBAND: *I hate to say it, but this toast is tough, dear.*
WIFE: You're eating the plate, darling.

What's grey and white and red all over?
An embarrassed elephant.

What do you give an elephant with big feet?
Plenty of room.

Why do elephants have big ears?
Because Noddy wouldn't pay the ransom.

What do you call an elephant wearing ear muffs?
Anything you like — he can't hear you!

Mac the Monster came stomping into the kitchen.
 'Where's my elephant stew?' he demanded. 'Where's my tooth sharpener? Where's my axe? Where's my—'
 'Hang on,' said his wife. 'I've only got three hands.'

'What's the difference between a loaf of bread and an elephant?'
'I don't know. What?'
'Well, I'm certainly not sending you out for a loaf of bread.'

What did the little grape say when the big elephant trod on it?
Nothing, it just gave out a little whine (wine).

How do you get down off an elephant?
You don't, you get down off a duck.

Why do elephants wear dark glasses?
If you had all these jokes told about you, you wouldn't want to be recognised either!

NINE STAR JOKES

Nine cheerful and cheeky CHIMPANZEES hope to make you chuckle at their favourite jokes....

Did you hear about the formal dance at the circus?
The penguins came in dinner jackets and the chimps wore their tails.

What was the chimps' favourite book?
'Ten Years in the Monkey House' by Bab Boone.

How did the chimpanzee escape from his cage?
He used a monkey wrench.

What did the banana do when the chimpanzee chased it?
The banana split.

What keys won't open doors?
Mon-keys.

'I like your new dog. Is he clever?'
   'Certainly! When I say to him "Are you coming for a walk or aren't you?" he either comes or he doesn't!'

What fruit would a chimp like to sleep on?
An ape-ri-cot.

How do you make a Venetian blind?
Poke a finger in his eye.

What has a big mouth but can't talk?
A jar.

DAD: *Come on, Denis, I'll take you to the circus.*
DENIS: If the circus want me, let them come and get me!

What is the best thing to take when you are run over?
The car's number.

A man was carving cold meat when some of it fell on the floor. It was just a slip of the tongue.

CANNIBAL CHIEF'S WIFE (to friend): Be sure to drop in for
   dinner tonight. We're having the Joneses for dinner.

What sort of monkey has a sweet tooth?
A meringue-outang.

What is a laser?
It's what a Chinaman shaves with.

Knock, knock,
Who's there?
The Avon lady. Your doorbell's broken.

What has a neck, two sides, a bottom and often a broken life?
A bottle.

The teacher visited Kenneth's house and asked if his mother was in.
 'She ain't in,' said Kenneth.
 'Why Kenneth! Where's your grammar?' exclaimed the teacher.
 'She ain't in neither,' said Kenneth.

'I got involved in a narrow squeak.'
'What did you do?'
'I trod on a mouse.'

What Christmas decorations do astronauts put in their space rockets?
Missile-toe.

Why couldn't anyone find the famous composer?
Because he was Haydn.

What kind of song do you sing in a car?
A cartoon (car tune).

What age is most important to a car?
The mile-age.

Did you hear about the tree surgeon who fell out of his patient?

What is a twip?
A twip is what a wabbit takes when he wides in a twain.

How do you stop a dog barking in the back seat of a car?
Put him in the front seat.

'Waiter! What's this worm on my plate?'
'That's your sausage, sir.'

What is a ghoul's favourite food?
Ghoulash.

CUSTOMER: *Waiter, is this a lamb chop or a pork chop?*
WAITER: Can't you tell the difference?
CUSTOMER: *No.*
WAITER: What's the matter then?

Who is always being let down by his mates?
A deep-sea diver.

Why should you stay calm when you meet a cannibal?
You don't want to get into a stew.

Why are mountain climbers curious?
They always want to take another peak (peek).

CHIP: *Look, there's a baby snake.*
MONK: How do you know it's a baby?
CHIP: *I can tell by its rattle.*

LITTLE BOY: *Will you pull a rabbit out of your hat?*
MAGICIAN: Sorry, Sonny, but I've just washed my hare, and I can't do a thing with it.

Why can't a bicycle stand up by itself?
Because it is two-tyred (too tired).

KENN: *Ouch! That water burned my hand.*
LENN: You should have felt it before you put your hand in.

What did the big cracker say to the little cracker?
My pop's bigger than your pop.

Why does the ringmaster in a circus wear red, white and blue braces?
To keep his trousers up.

Why is it fun to be an angel?
Because when you get to heaven you have a high old time.

Which animal has got wooden legs?
A timber wolf.

Why is cream more expensive than milk?
Because it's harder for cows to sit on small cartons.

What did the police do when two hundred hares escaped from the rabbit farm?
They combed the area.

Why needn't you take your watch with you when you fly in an aeroplane?
Because time flies anyway.

ONE SKELETON TO ANOTHER: If we had any guts we'd get out of this circus.

SEAL: *I want to join the army.*
SERGEANT: What's your name?
SEAL: *Fish, sir.*
SERGEANT: O.K. You can go in a tank.

What did the two flies on Robinson Crusoe's knee say?
'Bye-bye for now, I'll see you on Friday.'

A man was knocked over by a hit-and-run driver. As he got to his feet his friend asked him:
 'Did you get the number?'
 'No,' he replied, 'but I'd know that laugh again anywhere.'

When does a bishop keep doubtful company?
When he walks around with a crook.

If there were ten cats in a boat and one jumped out, how many would there be?
None, because they were all copy cats.

Have you heard about the amazing new discovery?
It is a pill that's half glue and half aspirin. It's for people with splitting headaches.

What is the hardest thing about learning to skate?
The ice.

DOCTOR: *Is your cough better?*
SAMMY: It ought to be, I've been practising all night.

What is the vampire's favourite song?
'Fangs for the memory.'

TEACHER: *Take this sentence: 'Let the cow be taken to the pasture', now – what mood?*
JOHNNY: The cow, sir.

What happened when the two lice moved to a new address?
They decided to give a louse-warming party.

Which artist had an arresting personality?
Constable.

LITTLE BOY: *Dad, where was I born?*
DAD: In London.
LITTLE BOY: *Where was Mum born?*
DAD: In Chicago.
LITTLE BOY: *Where were you born?*
DAD: In Paris.
LITTLE BOY: *It's amazing how we three came to meet.*

Knock, knock.
Who's there?
Boo.
Boo who?
There's no need to cry.

What is a cannibal's favourite soup?
One with plenty of body in it.

A fishmonger was putting up a sign outside his shop that said 'FRESH FISH SOLD HERE TODAY' when along came an elderly seal.

'Why put "TODAY", you won't be selling it tomorrow or yesterday, will you?' said the wise seal.

'No, I suppose not,' said the fishmonger.

'And you don't want "HERE" either – I mean,

you're not selling it anywhere else, are you?'

'No, you're dead right,' agreed the fishmonger.

'And then why put "SOLD", you're not giving it away, are you?'

'No.'

'And why say "FRESH" — you wouldn't sell it if it wasn't, would you?'

'I certainly wouldn't,' said the fishmonger. 'Thank you for saving me so much trouble.'

'It was no trouble,' said the seal, turning to go. 'And, by the way, you don't need "FISH" either — I could smell it two streets away!'

PATIENT: *Doctor, I've just swallowed a mouth-organ!*
DOCTOR: It's a good job you don't play the piano.

Who has more fun when you tickle a mule?
He may enjoy it, but you'll get a bigger kick out of it.

KENN: *How many sides has a circle?*
BENN: None.
KENN: *You're wrong. There are two – inside and outside.*

Did you hear about the bank clerk who climbed a tree because he wanted to become a branch manager?

'Stop the bus, an old lady's just fallen off!'
'It's all right, she's paid her fare.'

What should a girl wear if she wants to end a fight?
Make-up.

When do clocks die?
When their time is up.

Why is an expensive fur coat like a person who needs psychiatric treatment?
One is the minky kind, the other has a kinky mind.

MUM: *When you yawn you're supposed to put your hand to your mouth.*
BOY: What! And get bitten!

Who can shave three times a day and still have a beard?
A barber.

Why did the fly fly?
Because the spider spied her.

What sheet cannot be folded?
A sheet of ice.

OLD LADY: My memory is excellent. There are only three things I can't remember. I can't remember names, I can't remember faces, and I've forgotten what the third thing is.

How many chimneys does Father Christmas have to climb down?
Stacks.

'Waiter, why have you got your thumb on my steak?'
'I don't want it to fall off the plate again.'

'I say, waiter, this water is cloudy!'
'The water's all right, sir, it's the glass that's dirty.'

MAN: *What are you doing in my tree?*
BOY: One of your apples fell off and I'm just putting it back.

MAN AT CONTROL TOWER: *Please state your height and position.*
PILOT: I'm five feet ten inches tall and I'm sitting in the cockpit.

Knock, knock.
Who's there?
Dismay.
Dismay who?
Dismay be a joke but it doesn't make me laugh.

'*I say, your puppy just bit me on the ankle!*'
'Well, he's not big enough to bite you on the neck.'

CUSTOMER: *When you sold me this cat you told me it would be splendid for mice – but it won't go near them.*
PETSHOP OWNER: Well, isn't that splendid for the mice?

What goes 200 mph on a washing line?
Honda pants.

Knock, knock.
Who's there?
Cows.
Cows who?
Cows go moo, not who.

SIGN OUTSIDE A CINEMA:
Showing now: *The Strongmen*, featuring Samson, Hercules, Goliath. ALL WEAK.

What washing powder does Kojak use?
Bald automatic.

What did the jack say to the car?
Let me give you a lift.

After the flood Noah and his wife were clearing out the Ark. They lined up the animals two by two, and Noah led them down the gangway, saying,
 'Go forth and multiply.'
The elephants marched off, followed by the bears and the tigers. Then the chimpanzees and the donkeys started arguing.
 'Why are you chimps trying to get in front of the donkeys?' demanded Noah.
 'You told us to go fourth,' said the chimps, 'and so we didn't want to go fifth.'
Finally Noah got them sorted out and soon everyone was out of the Ark, except two snakes who were crying in the corner.
 'Didn't you hear me say go forth and multiply?' asked Noah.
 'Yes, but we can't,' wailed the snakes, 'we're adders.'

How does a boat show its affection?
It hugs the shore.

VILMA VAMPIRE: *This tramp came to me and said he hadn't had a bite for days.*
VICTOR VAMPIRE: So what did you do?
VILMA VAMPIRE: *I bit him.*

When does a man become two men?
When he is beside himself.

What did the man do when he got his gas bill?
He exploded!

TEN STAR JOKES

And now, the moment you've been waiting for. . . .
Top of the bill at the Big Top!
Those ten comical, crazy CLOWNS climb into the circus ring to present their own special favourites. . . .

Why are clowns like an operation?
They both have you in stitches.

Bobo clown was looking for somewhere to water-ski, but gave up when he couldn't find a sloping lake.

How can you tell the difference between a tin of soup and a tin of baked beans?
Read the label.

KENNY: *How long does it take to get from London to Birmingham?*
LENNY: About two hours.
KENNY: *How long from Birmingham to London?*
LENNY: The same, you fool. You should know that.
KENNY: *Why? It's not the same from Easter to Christmas as it is from Christmas to Easter.*

Why is a fish like a person who talks too much?
Because it can't keep its mouth shut.

What fruit goes around in couples?
Pears.

JOJO: *Did you see the parade passing by?*
TOTO: No, I was waving my hair at the time.
JOJO: *That's funny. I was waving a flag.*

BOBO CLOWN: *I spend half my time trying to be witty.*
BIBI CLOWN: Yes, you're a half-wit!

BENNY: *What time is it?*
KENNY: Three o'clock.
BENNY: *Oh, no! Not again!*
KENNY: What's the matter?
BENNY: *I've been asking people the time all day and everyone tells me something different!*

NONO: *Do you realise it takes three sheep to make one jumper?*
MOMO: I didn't even know that sheep could knit.

BOBO: *Do you live in a small house?*
BIBI: I should say! It's so small even the mice are round-shouldered.

KENNY CLOWN: *Doctor, I've swallowed a mouse. What shall I do?*
DOCTOR: Wave a piece of cheese in front of your mouth.

DOCTOR: *Why are you waving that sardine in front of your mouth?*
KENNY: I've swallowed a cat!

When does a chair dislike you?
When it can't bear you.

NONO: *Why is my piece of pie all smashed?*
MOMO: Well, you said 'Fetch me a piece of pie, and step on it'.

ROMEO: *I am only a pebble in your life.*
JULIET: Why don't you try being a little boulder?

117

MAD CLOWN: *Where are you going with that manure?*
FARMER: I'm going to put it on my strawberries.
MAD CLOWN: *And they say I'm crazy! I always put cream on mine.*

NONO: *Don't fall into that pond, it's about ten feet deep.*
LOLO: Ten feet? But it only reaches up to the middle of those ducks.

If it takes ten clowns forty-five minutes to eat a ham, how long will it take twenty clowns to eat half a ham?
It depends on whether they are professional clowns or 'am-a-chewers'!

What did one casket say to the other casket?
Is that you coffin?

BOBO: *Do you still walk in your sleep?*
JOJO: Not since I dropped tin-tacks on the floor.

LOLO: *Do you like my new suit? I got it for a ridiculous price.*
TOTO: You mean you got it for an absurd figure.

NONO: *Where's your dog?*
TOTO: I had him put down.
NONO: *Was he mad?*
TOTO: Well, he wasn't too pleased about it.

What kind of cup does not hold water?
A cupcake.

Did you hear about the clown making pancakes?
He put sugar on his head and scratched his pancakes.

TOTO: *Do you say 'nine and five is thirteen', or 'nine and five are thirteen'?*
BOBO: Nine and five *are* thirteen.
TOTO: *No they're not, nine and five are fourteen.*

What was the name of the engineer's wife?
Bridget (Bridge it).

What do you get if you cross a donkey with mother?
Ass-ma.

BOBO: *Our dog is a great watchdog. We always know when a stranger comes.*
BIBI: *Why? Does he bark and growl if someone comes?*
BOBO: *No, he crawls under the bed.*

Did you hear about the writer who dropped seven stories into a waste-paper basket and lived?

'What happens if the parachute doesn't open?' asked the clown about to jump from an aeroplane for the first time.
    'That,' said the pilot, 'is what we call jumping to a conclusion.'

Why did the one-handed man cross the road?
To go to the second-hand shop.

Why was Lassie a famous dog in films?
Because she was always given the lead.

FIRST CLOWN: *I'm always very careful about washing my hands.*
SECOND CLOWN: Why?
FIRST CLOWN: *Well, I don't want them to go rusty.*

'*Mum, there's a man at the door collecting for the Old Folks' Home.*'
'*Give him your Grandma.*'

Where do you take a sick wasp?
To waspital.

TOTO: *When I sat down to play the piano everybody laughed.*
JOJO: Why?
TOTO: *No bench.*

What happened to the man who stole a calendar?
He got twelve months.

What's the best system of book-keeping?
Never lend them.

What flower does everyone have?
Tulips (two lips).

What did the snake-charmer and the undertaker get for wedding-presents?
Two towels marked 'Hiss' and 'Hearse'.

What do you call a Scottish cloakroom attendant?
Angus MacMacup.

Why did the teacher wear dark glasses?
Because the class was so bright.

JOJO: *What is the difference between you and a forger?*
TOTO: I give up.
JOJO: *You try to make the funny, he tries to make the money.*

NONO: *I wish you'd only sing Christmas Carols.*
MOMO: Why?
NONO: *You'd only sing once a year then!*

Laugh and the world laughs with you; weep and your mother takes your temperature.

KENNY: *This suit fits me like a glove.*
BENNY: Pity it doesn't fit you like a suit.

What is the difference between a burglar and a man wearing a wig?
One has false keys, one has false locks.

What do you get if you cross a pig with the M1?
A road hog.

Why does a pencil seem heavy when you write with it for a long time?
Because it is full of lead.

If ten clowns, two chimps, one seal and an elephant stand under one umbrella, why don't any of them get wet?
Because it isn't raining.

How was the tall clown made short?
The white-faced clown borrowed £50 from him.

Did you hear about the two clowns who got stuck in a revolving door?
They're still going around together.

What did the Welsh clown call his apple?
A Taffy apple.

What did the doctor say when he met a fellow doctor?
'You're looking fine. How am I?'

BENNY CLOWN: *Kenny, how do you spell 'rain'?*
KENNY CLOWN: R-A-N-E.
BENNY CLOWN: *That's the worst spell of rain we've had around here for a long time.*

'What did you get for your birthday?'
'A year older.'

Did you hear about the ship with twenty-five tons of yo-yos on board that crossed the Pacific?
It sank forty-two times.

What did one wall say to the other?
I'll meet you at the corner.

BOBO: *Keep your dog away from me!*
BIBI: Don't you know the old proverb 'A barking dog never bites'?
BOBO: *Yes, but does your dog know the proverb?*

What's green and goes 'Boing, boing, boing'?
Spring cabbage.

TOTO CLOWN: My grandmother's very strange. Even on the coldest nights she goes out and gets coal in her nightie. I bought her a shovel, but she says her nightie holds more.

NONO: *What would you do if you locked yourself out of your caravan?*
MOMO: I'd keep singing until I found the right key.

123

BOBO: *How did you break your leg?*
BIBI: *I put my cigarette in an open manhole and then stepped on it.*

What do you have to do to stop a mad doctor following you?
Carry an apple.

What do you get if you cross a watchdog with a werewolf?
A very nervous postman.

How do clowns dress on a cold day?
Quickly.

What did one arithmetic book say to another arithmetic book?
'Boy, do I have problems.'

Who was the fastest runner in the world?
Adam, because he was first in the human race.

Will you remember me in a month?
Certainly.
Will you remember me in a year?
Of course.
Will you remember me in two years?
Yes.
Will you remember me in three years?
Of course I will!
Knock, knock.
Who's there?
See, you've forgotten me already.

Knock, knock.
Who's there?
Major.
Major who?
Major answer, didn't I?

Why is a Scottish boy with a cold like a soldier with seven days' leave.
Because they both have a wee cough (week off).

What is yellow and white and travels at 100 mph along a railway line?
A train driver's egg sandwich.

Where does the lamb go when he wants a hair cut?
To the baa-baa shop.

PATIENT: *Doctor, Doctor, can you help me out?*
DOCTOR: Certainly, which way did you come in?

TEACHER: *You can't sleep in class.*
GIRL: No. But if you didn't talk so loud I could.

Who's the world's biggest stinker?
King-Pong.

When an apple hits a banana in the mouth, what is it called?
A fruit punch.

'*Waiter, are these eggs fresh?*'
'Fresh! Why, the hens haven't even missed them yet.'

What did the big hand say to the little hand?
Got a minute?

OPTICIAN: *Have your eyes recently been checked?*
WOMAN: No, they've always been blue.

WOMAN (on telephone): *What's the weather like where you are?*
DAUGHTER: It's so hot the cows are giving evaporated milk.

If a fat man fell down the stairs, what would he fall against?
Against his wishes.

DOCTOR: *The pain in your right leg is caused by old age.*
OLD MAN: But my left leg is the same age and that doesn't hurt.

How do you spell 'dried grass' in three letters?
H-A-Y.

Why was the ocean uncomfortable?
Because he had crabs in his bed.

'*Do these stairs take you to the second floor?*'
'No. I'm afraid you have to walk.'

JOKE BOOKS

If you enjoyed reading all the hilarious jokes in this book, perhaps you ought to try some more of our zany joke books. They are available in bookshops or they can be ordered directly from us. Just complete the form below and enclose the right amount of money and the books will be sent to you at home.

☐	THE WOOLLY JUMPER JOKE BOOK	Peter Eldin	£1.25
☐	MORE BROWNIE JOKES		£1.25
☐	THE WOBBLY JELLY JOKE BOOK	Jim Eldridge	£1.25
☐	A VERY MICE JOKE BOOK	John Hegarty	£1.25
☐	THE JOKE-A-DAY FUN BOOK	Janet Rogers	£1.50
☐	THE CRAZY JOKE BOOK STRIKES BACK	Janet Rogers	£1.50
☐	THE ELEPHANT JOKE BOOK	Katie Wales	£1.00
☐	FLOELLA'S FUNNIEST JOKES	Floella Benjamin	£1.25

If you would like to order books, please send this form, and the money due to:
ARROW BOOKS, BOOKSERVICE BY POST, PO BOX 29, DOUGLAS, ISLE OF MAN, BRITISH ISLES. Please enclose a cheque or postal order made out to Arrow Books Ltd for the amount due including 30p per book for postage and packing both for orders within the UK and for overseas orders.

NAME ....

ADDRESS ....

....

Please print clearly.